The purpose of this study guide is to provide supplemental educational material. It is not intended as a substitute or replacement of JUST MERCY.

Published by SuperSummary, www.supersummary.com

ISBN – 9781074918392

For more information or to learn about our complete library of study guides, please visit http://www.supersummary.com

Please submit any comments, corrections, or questions to:
http://www.supersummary.com/support/

TABLE OF CONTENTS

PLOT OVERVIEW   **2**

CHAPTER SUMMARIES AND ANALYSES   **6**

Introduction- Chapter 3   6
Chapter 4-6   12
Chapter 7-10   17
Chapter 11-13   24
Chapter 14-Epilogue   27

MAJOR CHARACTER ANALYSIS   **34**

Bryan Stevenson
Walter McMillian
Ralph Myers
Sherriff Tate

THEMES   **39**

SYMBOLS AND MOTIFS   **43**

IMPORTANT QUOTES   **46**

ESSAY TOPICS   **55**

Part memoir, part exhortation for much-needed reform to the American criminal justice system, Bryan Stevenson's Just Mercy is a heartrending and inspirational call to arms written by the activist lawyer who founded the Equal Justice Initiative, an Alabama-based organization responsible for freeing or reducing the sentences of scores of wrongfully convicted individuals. Stevenson's memoir weaves together personal stories from his years as a lawyer with strong statements against racial and legal injustice, drawing a clear through line from Antebellum slavery and its legacy to today's still-prejudiced criminal justice system.

Between the 1970s and 2014, when Stevenson's memoir was published, the U.S. prison population increased from 300,000 to 2,300,000 – the highest incarceration rate in the world. Of those incarcerated, 58 percent identify as Black or Hispanic. The War on Drugs and "Tough on Crime" policing policies disproportionately target juveniles, women, people of color, the poor, and individuals with mental health issues, all too often the victims of inflated sentences and wrongful convictions resulting in the death penalty. Stevenson animates these harrowing statistics with stories from his years as a criminal defense lawyer, personalizing the political through a powerful series of cases.

The narrative backbone is the story of Walter McMillian, a young black man falsely accused of murdering a white woman in the small southern town where To Kill a Mockingbird is set. Chapters alternate between chronicling his trial, conviction, and the long road to justice and recounting the stories of other wrongfully persecuted individuals, including a 14-year old named Charlie who is sentenced to life in prison without parole for killing his mother's abusive boyfriend. Taken as a whole, Just Mercy asks readers to consider the notion that the opposite of poverty is not wealth – it is justice.

By the start of the first chapter, "Mockingbird Players", Stevenson is a member of the bar in both Georgia and Alabama, and has found himself defending McMillian for the murder of 18-year old Ronda Morrison. While there is no solid evidence pointing to McMillian as the murderer, false accusations, political machinations, and implicit bias against a black man known to be involved in an adulterous interracial relationship all add up to the accusation sticking.

The chapters that focus on cases outside of McMillian's demonstrate the staggering legal injustices delivered upon marginalized populations and expose the larger, systemic causes and institutionalized prejudice at work in their uneven treatment.

Chapter 2, "Stand" details several incidents of police brutality and racial profiling, including an encounter Stevenson himself had while listening to music in front of his apartment late one night.

Chapter 4, "Old Rugged Cross", describes the story of Vietnam War veteran Herbert Richardson, whose case illuminates the struggles Veterans often have in obtaining the medical and mental health support they need, while Chapter 6 ("Surely Doomed") depicts how widespread legal injustice is for juveniles, many of whom are tried and convicted as adults and receive much harsher sentences than they deserve.

Chapter 8 introduces readers to Tracy, Ian, and Antonio, who continue Stevenson's exploration of incarcerated children, in these cases for non-homicidal offenses. Through their stories, Stevenson exposes the truth about how children of color are often incarcerated or worse for the same acts white children engage in with impunity. At fourteen, Antonio Nunez became the youngest person in U.S. history to be condemned to death for a crime in which no one was physically injured.

Chapter 10, "Mitigation," turns its critical lens on the poor and mentally ill prison population, who –though corrections officers are not properly trained to handle mental health issues – make up more than half of those currently incarcerated. The case-in-point in this chapter is Avery Jenkins, who committed murder during a psychotic episode. Through Stevenson's interventions, he is ultimately moved to a mental health facility better equipped to care for him, one step closer to a society that chooses to rehabilitate rather than incarcerate.

Chapter 12 touches upon impoverished women imprisoned for infant mortality beyond their control, and welfare reform designed to persecute poor, single mothers, and Chapter 14 focuses on physically, cognitively, and behaviorally disabled children who end up imprisoned. Chapter 16 ends on a hopeful note, as on May 17, 2010, the U.S. Supreme Court announced that sentences of life imprisonment without parole imposed on children convicted of non-homicidal crimes was cruel and unusual punishment.

The chapters that trace the unfolding of Walter McMillian's case build a narrative arc between the late 1980s, when McMillian was accused, and his eventual release in 1993. According to Stevenson's account, the case involves countless missteps, including sentencing McMillian to the death penalty before his trial officially began, moving the trial proceedings to a wealthier, and thereby whiter, community, where McMillian was less likely to be judged by a jury of his peers, and ignoring several eyewitness accounts that definitively gave the defendant an alibi. Police misconduct (including a paid testimony), perjury, witnesses flipping, and rejected appeals to the state circuit courts also created setbacks. After less than three hours of deliberation, and despite his obvious innocence, the jury found McMillian guilty of the murder of Ronda Morrison and sentenced him to death.

Late-breaking assistance from the television show 60 Minutes raised awareness of the dubiousness of McMillian's case, and convinced the Monroe County district attorney to bring in the Alabama Bureau of Investigation (ABI). Ultimately, the court ruled in favor of McMillian, and after six years on death row, he was released and cleared of all charges. McMillian became a cause célèbre for criminal justice reform, resulting in the Equal Justice Initiative being selected for an International Human Rights Award.

Chapter 15, "Broken", ends with an impassioned plea for a reevaluation of the ethics of capital punishment. By 1999, increasing media coverage of the high rate of wrongful convictions finally began to lessen reliance on the death penalty. In the closing chapter of *Just Mercy*, the lesson Stevenson impresses upon his readers is the urgent need to acknowledge the brokenness of society-wide indifference to the most vulnerable populations in America. Criminal justice reform must begin and end with mercy.

Introduction- Chapter 3

Introduction Summary: Higher Ground

In 1983, Bryan Stevenson is a 23-year-old Harvard Law student. He grew in a "poor, rural, racially segregated settlement" (12) in Delaware, a place where white people displayed Confederate flags despite living in a former Union state. Black families like Stevenson's were excluded and marginalized. His grandmother, the daughter of former slaves, reminds Stevenson that he must stay close to his heritage—he cannot learn about anything from a distance.

Despite having no real background in law, Bryan decided to obtain a law degree as a means to solving racial injustice in America. He found his classes at Harvard Law School to be overly academic, "disconnected from the race and poverty issues that had motivated [Stevenson] to consider the law in the first place" (4). In the summer before his third and final year, Stevenson takes a position as an intern for the Southern Prisoners Defense Committee, an organization designed to support and aid prisoners, particularly those on death row. One day, Stevenson is asked to visit a Georgian death row prisoner. The SPDC does not yet have a lawyer available, so Stevenson is sent to communicate one thing to this prisoner, named Henry: *"You will not be killed in the next year"* (7).

Stevenson is nervous, having never met a man on death row before, but Henry greets him happily, overjoyed to hear he will not receive an execution date for at least another year. They spend three hours talking about everything—both case-related and personal. Stevenson has overstayed the visiting hours, and the prison guards are annoyed. As they roughly take Henry away, Henry begins singing "Higher Ground," a Christian hymn Stevenson knows well from childhood Sundays. "In that moment," Stevenson says, "Henry altered my understanding of human potential, redemption, and hopefulness" (12).

Stevenson now sets up the aim of *Just Mercy*: he will use his former cases to paint a picture of the American legal system and the terrible consequences mass incarceration and the death penalty has had on life in the United States.

Chapter 1 Summary: Mockingbird Players

It is now 1988. Stevenson is now a full-fledged lawyer still working for the SPDC. He receives a call from an Alabama judge named Robert E. Lee Key—the fact that he is named after a Confederate general is not lost on Stevenson. Judge Key has heard that Stevenson plans to represent a man named Walter McMillian, a black man on death row for the murder of a white woman. Judge Key tries to persuade Stevenson not to take the case—Walter is a major drug dealer, Judge Key says, before asking if Stevenson is even a member of the Alabama bar association, given that he lives in Georgia. Stevenson is. Judge Key does not believe Walter is truly poor, either, and therefore not in need of free legal services. Stevenson is undeterred. He has already met Walter, who is adamant that he is innocent of murder. Stevenson chooses to believe him.

After the call with Judge Key, Stevenson reviews the evidence in Walter's case. The murder trial was short. Walter was born and raised in Monroeville, Alabama, the birthplace of author Harper Lee and the approximate setting of her famous novel *To Kill a Mockingbird*. The novel's plot involves a black man named Tom Robinson who is falsely accused and convicted of raping a white woman. He is shot while attempting a prison break. Stevenson notes that despite these themes of racial injustice and white violence, Monroeville remains a deeply segregated, deeply racist place. Walter grew up in a sharecropping family before starting his own business. Unhappy in his marriage, he began an affair with a local (married) white woman, Karen Kelly. The interracial affair created a local scandal, and Stevenson notes the long history of public opposition to black-white romantic relationships in America.

Shortly after the affair came to light, a white teenager named Ronda Morrison was found murdered in normally sleepy Monroeville. Ronda was the daughter of a prominent local family, and the police felt pressure to close the case despite no good leads. The police eventually targeted Ralph Myers, a drug-using white man with a lengthy criminal record. Ralph was involved romantically with Karen Kelly, whom Walter was now trying to break up with. Ralph and Karen had been implicated in the death of a different white woman named Vickie Pittman. During interrogations, Ralph stated that Walter had been involved in Vickie's murder as well, and that Walter *alone* had killed Ronda. There was no actual evidence against Walter, however—Ralph couldn't even pick him out an informal lineup.

Chapter 2 Summary: Stand

Stevenson recounts the events of his first years working for the SPDC. To survive on his small salary, he moves in with a friend from Harvard, a "white kid from North Carolina" (35) named Charlie. As he works, he begins to plan a new law project to represent death row inmates in Alabama, which executes a shocking number of people each year— almost all men, most black. Meanwhile, he takes cases about prisoner abuse at Southern jails and prisons. In one case, a man brought in on a traffic violation is beaten by guards and denied his asthma inhaler. The man dies. In another case, a black teenage boy is shot after running a red light. The police claim he was reaching for a gun. He was reaching for his driver's license.

One night, Stevenson arrives at his apartment complex after a long, grueling day of work. He listens to his favorite song on the radio—"Stand!" by Sly and the Family Stone. He notices a police presence on his block and decides to go into his apartment. When he opens his car door, a police officer points a loaded weapon at him. Stevenson is terrified but remains compliant and calm as the officers throw him against the car and illegally search it. Finding nothing, they release him. "'We're letting you go. You should be happy,'" (42) one officer says. Stevenson files an official complaint but is condescendingly brushed off. He decides to begin speaking to youth groups, church groups, and community organizations about demanding police accountability. After one talk, he is approached by an older man in a wheelchair. The man was involved in the Civil Rights Movement of the 1960s and shows Stevenson all his scars from police brutality—he calls them "medals of honor" (46). After this encounter, Steven resolves to open his own Alabama office.

Chapter 3 Summary: Trials and Tribulations

Stevenson returns to the facts of Walter's case. Despite no evidence against Walter other than Ralph Myers' shoddy testimony, Walter is arrested. The charge is sodomy— Ralph also accused Walter of raping him, and anti-homosexuality laws allow him to be held. Sherriff Tate laces his interrogation of Walter with racial slurs and references to a lynching in Mobile three years previous. Law enforcements sees all the holes in Ralph's story, so find Bill Hooks, a local jailhouse snitch, to say he saw Walter's distinctive truck near the crime scene. Walter is indicted for the murder, and the local white community reacts with "joy and relief" (50). Black residents, some of whom saw Walter at a fish fry at the time of the murder, tell the Sherriff the wrong man was arrested, but they are ignored. Ralph, seeing how serious this has become, tries to recant. Both Ralph and Walter are held on death row at Holman prison, despite this being illegal for pretrial defendants.

Living conditions in Holman are brutal. Ralph and Walter are locked in tiny cells for 23 hours a day. They must daily face the sight of the yellow electric chair, nicknamed Yellow Mama. They hear about grisly execution details from other inmates. Other inmates encourage Walter to file a complaint, but he is illiterate and so cannot. After Ralph experiences (from a distance, in his cell) his first execution, he has a mental collapse. Though he had previously refused to testify against Walter, he now reconsiders. Sherriff Tate agrees to move him from death row in exchange for testimony. Judge Key and District Attorney Bill Pearson conspire to move the trial from Monroe County (with a large black population) to Baldwin County, which is heavily white, despite the illegality of this act. Ralph once again recants. Tate sends him a local mental hospital, which deems him fit to testify. Ralph returns to death row at Holman and eventually agrees to testify.

The trial is brief. The DA uses all his jury selection strikes to exclude all but one black juror. Ralph's testimony is erratic and borderline nonsensical. Walter notes, with horror, that "Everyone seemed to be rushing to get the trial over with" (66). Despite obvious problems with witness testimony and a timeline that makes no sense, the jury finds Walter guilty.

Introduction-Chapter 3 Analysis

The first few chapters serve to provide the reader necessary context on both Bryan Stevenson and Walter McMillian. The men outwardly appear to be different. Stevenson is a young, idealistic, Ivy League-educated lawyer with the knowledge and determination to take on the criminal justice system. Walter is an older, illiterate man with a shaky past looking for nothing more than to escape the criminal justice system. And yet, within these first chapters, parallels between Stevenson and Walter become clear. They are both black men in a region and nation that discriminates against them in both obvious and insidious ways. Walter is framed for a murder he did not commit to appease the scared white community. Stevenson, for all his education and in-depth knowledge of the law, is unable to protect himself against racial profiling. Both men are, by virtue of nothing than their race, terrorized by a justice system that inherently thinks the worst of them. Both are bewildered by their treatment. Walter finds Ralph's testimony laughable, but the white jury does not. Stevenson is appalled when an officer tells him to be glad he wasn't arrested, despite the fact that he committed no crime, and is further appalled when his formal complaint is ignored. Though their circumstances may be different, their experiences as black American men have parallels, and contribute to the deep friendship they eventually forge.

Also present in this chapter is the long shadow of *To Kill a Mockingbird*, Harper Lee's famous novel about a wrongfully convicted black man. The parallels of this narrative to Walter's are obvious, but Stevenson goes deeper into analysis. He presents the white Monroeville community as hugely proud of Harper Lee as a native daughter and have even erected a museum to the novel. And yet, when a similar case presented itself in real life—

Walter McMillian's—the white community reacted much like townspeople of the fictional Maycomb. They agitate for justice for a white woman's murder and are content when Walter is offered up as a sacrifice. They are placated by this and ignore the inconsistencies in the trial testimony and the obvious pain of their black neighbors, who know Walter is innocent. Furthermore, as Stevenson notes, they are quick to hold *To Kill a Mockingbird* up as proof of their own racial tolerance while never noting how the fictional trial ends—the innocent black man "is shot seventeen times in the back by his captors" (23). Stevenson uses *To Kill a Mockingbird* to show two portraits of Monroeville's white community: the people they believe themselves to be, and the people they really are.

Chapter 4-6

Chapter 4 Summary: The Old Rugged Cross

In the summer of 1989, Stevenson and his friend Eva Ansley open the Alabama office he dreamed of—the Equal Justice Initiative, or EJI. They have little funds and almost no staff, but are almost instantly inundated with requests for help from death row inmates in Alabama. One of their clients is Michael Lindsey, whose former attorney, David Bagwell, had become disillusioned and written a screed about how mad dogs—that is, death row inmates—"'ought to die'" (69). Lindsey had originally been sentenced to life imprisonment by a jury, but a judge had changed the order to death. Stevenson and Eva Ansley argue that the jury's original sentence be imposed, but they are denied. Lindsey is executed. Another client is Horace Dunkins, who is severely intellectually disabled. The Supreme Court will not term the execution of mentally disabled people "cruel and unusual punishment" for another thirteen years. Dunkins is executed.

Stevenson receives a desperate call from another man on death row, Herbert Richardson. Herbert is a Vietnam War veteran who was traumatized by the war. He attempted suicide multiple times before landing in a mental hospital, where he fell in love with a nurse. After their relationship turned toxic, the nurse left him and moved home to Alabama. Herbert followed her and left a bomb on her front porch, hoping the explosion would cause he to return to him for protection and comfort. Instead, the bomb ended up killing her ten-year-old niece, and Herbert was sentenced to death for that murder. Stevenson argues that Herbert never meant to kill anyone, and that the jury was unduly influenced by a poor defense and the prosecution's totally unsubstantiated claim that Herbert was a Black Muslim. His lawyer ignored Herbert's desire to appeal the sentence. Despite Stevenson's best efforts, Herbert's execution sentence is upheld. Not even the victim's family—who explicitly do not want Herbert killed—can change the outcome.

Stevenson goes to be with Herbert and his family on the day of the execution. A final stay of execution is denied. A corrections officer, visibly shaken, arrives to take Herbert to his death. The moment is "a flood of sadness and tragedy" (86). Herbert had requested the hymn "The Old Rugged Cross" be played as he walked to the electric chair, and Stevenson and the family begin humming it. Herbert and Stevenson pray together. It is the first time Stevenson witnesses an execution.

Chapter 5 Summary: Of the Coming of John

Stevenson goes to meet with Walter's immediate family, including his long-suffering wife, Minnie, and their daughter, Jackie. The McMillian house is in a state of "profound disrepair" and is clearly "a poor family's home"

(93). They discuss the trial before—to Stevenson's surprise—introducing him to Walter's 30-person extended family down the road. He sends them love and well wishes from Walter, and they all talk long into the night about the case and what an appeal will entail. He senses that the meeting has given them a sense of hope where there was once only despair.

As he drives back home, Stevenson thinks of the W.E.B. DuBois short story "On the Coming of John." In this story, a poor black community in Georgia pools money to send its most promising young man, named John, to a teacher's college up north. He returns after graduation and starts a school for black children focused on empowerment and racial equality. The local white community, feeling threatened, wants the school closed. A white judge orders it shut down. That very day, a distraught John witnesses the judge's son sexually assaulting John's sister. Enraged, John strikes the judge's son with a piece of wood and is killed by a lynch mob. Stevenson, the first in his family to attend college, identifies with John "as the hope of entire community" (100).

Stevenson grows closer to Walter and the two become real friends. Stevenson receives a call from Darnell Houston, who says he can prove of the trial's key witnesses, a man named Bill Hooks, was lying. Darnell was with Bill at the time Bill claims to have seen Walter near the murder scene. Knowing it's a long short, Stevenson petitions for an entirely new trial. Darnell is arrested for "perjury," but it is clearly simple retaliation for talking to Stevenson. Stevenson meets with the new DA, Tom Chapman. Chapman seems unconcerned with issues of bias and perjury in Walter's trial—Walter made the local white community angry, and that was enough. Stevenson sees that Chapman is "either naïve or wilfully indifferent—or worse" (109). Chapman tells Stevenson that Judge Key has already denied the motion for a new trial. On his way out of the office, Stevenson is outraged to see yet another flyer for the local theater's production of *To Kill a Mockingbird*.

Chapter 6 Summary: Surely Doomed

One late night, Stevenson receives a call from an old woman in Virginia. She tells him that her fourteen-year-old grandson, Charlie, has been in an adult jail for two days on a murder charge. She is in poor health and unable to see him. Stevenson explains that EJI works on death penalty cases, which Charlie's is not—the Supreme Court recently forbade the execution of those convicted of crimes while under the age of fifteen. She begs him and prays. He agrees to go see Charlie.

Charlie, Stevenson learns, killed his mother's abusive boyfriend after the boyfriend nearly murdered her in cold blood. Since the boyfriend was a police officer, the prosecutor intended to try Charlie as an adult and had him sent to an adult facility. When Stevenson meets Charlie—tiny and less than 100 pounds—Charlie reveals he has been raped by several inmates. Stevenson is outraged that this was allowed to occur. Stevenson has Charlie moved first to a single cell, then to a juvenile facility. Over time, Charlie recovers, though he is forever "tormented by what he'd done and what he'd been through" (124).

After telling Charlie's story to a church group, Stevenson is approached by an older white couple—Mr. and Mrs. Jennings. Their only grandchild committed suicide, and they want to donate his college fund to help care for Charlie, whose grandmother has since died and whose mother is struggling financially. The Jenningses support

Charlie as he obtains his GED while in prison, and are there with his mother the day he is released.

Chapter 4-6 Analysis

This section is notable in its painful, harrowing depictions of the lives and deaths of vulnerable people. Stevenson takes the reader through execution, the McMillian home, and the life of a traumatized child in visceral detail. In "The Old Rugged Cross" readers are given a moment-by-moment account of Herbert Richardson's last day. Stevenson refuses to spare the reader anything. We see Herbert's hysterical wife, the great sadness of those gathered, the discomfort of the guards who find themselves complicit in the execution, and Herbert's own fear and dread. In doing so, the reader is given an opportunity few have: to witness—through Stevenson's eyes—an American execution. "I couldn't stop thinking," Stevenson writes, "that we don't spend much time contemplating the details of what killing someone actually involves" (90). This revelation informs the way Stevenson constructs Chapter 4. Readers see, as much as they can secondhand, just what an act of capital punishment entails. If they are proponents of this practice, they must now grapple with this new knowledge. It is raw and horrifying to read, just as Stevenson intended.

Stevenson continues this trend of detail-heavy, emotionally difficult scenes in Chapter 6. He describes first the context of Charlie's traumatic childhood and the abuse he witnessed and endured. He then takes the reader through his first meeting with Charlie. While Stevenson could easily have skipped the awkward, confusing, and maddeningly slow first hour of their meeting, he chooses not to do this. By describing each moment, each attempt on his part to open Charlie up, and his own panic over not being able to connect with an obviously traumatized child, Stevenson encourages us to experience these feelings *with* him. When Charlie ultimately breaks down, it is all the more real for the reader, and all the more painful. In this section, Stevenson refuses to let the reader off the hook. He refuses to sanitize his experiences or spare the reader the most painful details. It is this lack of distance that makes *Just Mercy* so powerful.

Chapter 7-10

Chapter 7 Summary: Justice Denied

All of Stevenson's appeals on Walter's behalf are denied. He was before Judge Patterson, a notorious former opponent of Civil Rights and school integration who is backed by the KKK. After the appeals are denied, Stevenson tries to encourage Walter to remain hopeful. Stevenson hires Michael O'Connor, a first-generation American who grew up in a rough Philadelphia neighborhood doing drugs but is now a Yale-educated lawyer. Stevenson and Michael investigate Walter's case further and find more inconsistencies and suspicious circumstances. They see evidence that Bill Hooks was paid off and his charges dropped in exchange for testimony against Walter. They find a flyer for the fish fry, indicating it was on the same day as the murder. Walter's distinctive truck—upon which Bill Hooks' testimony is based—was not modified until months *after* the murder. Ralph Myers calls Stevenson and begs to speak to him. Stevenson visits Myers in prison, where Myers explains he was coerced into giving false testimony and intimidated with threats of death row to maintain that testimony. He now wants to recant in court.

Michael and Stevenson follow up on the few leads Myers was able to provide. They visit Karen Kelly in prison, and she confirms that Myers and Walter never met. She tells them Sherriff Tate taunted and abused her for sleeping with black men. They look into Vickie Pittman's murder, all but forgotten in the wake of Ronda Morrison's murder. Vickie was from a poor, rural white family, and her two aunts feel as though she was seen as white trash and nothing else—unlike Ronda Morrison. The aunts have heard that Vickie's father might have been involved in her murder, as well as the corrupt local sheriff. Stevenson notes that though the lives of victims are given greater weight and care during criminal trials, not all victims are equal. Class, race, and occupation all contribute to how victims are perceived.

Stevenson and Michael file a Rule 32 petition, hoping for an eventual post-conviction collateral appeal. The Supreme Court of Alabama approves the petition, indicating that they too see the fishiness of this case. Stevenson and Michael are granted access to all the criminal files, including those of Sherriff Tate, the psych hospital Myers stayed at, and the Pittman files (they are from another county and were previously out of reach). Sherriff Tate and DA Chapman are quietly hostile towards them. "It wasn't long after that," Stevenson writes, "when the bomb threats started" (146).

Chapter 8 Summary: All God's Children

In this chapter, Stevenson highlights the cases of several imprisoned people convicted of crimes they committed as young children. They are all EPI clients Stevenson has tried to help. The first is Trina Garnett. As a young child with intellectual disabilities, she watched her drunken, abusive father beat her mother and siblings and kill her dog with a hammer. After her mother died, her father began sexually abusing her. At fourteen, she accidentally caused a fire that resulted in the death of two boys. She is prosecuted as an adult, and due to mandatory minimum sentence, the judge is forced to condemn her to life in prison despite his "serious misgivings" (150). At an adult women's prison, she is raped by a guard and becomes pregnant. She gives birth in shackles, her son is sent to foster care, and she receives no compensation for the crime against her.

The second case is that of Ian Manuel. Thirteen-year-old Ian shot a woman in the face during a botched robbery and was sentenced to life without parole. At an adult facility, he is held in solitary confinement so he will not be raped by older inmates. But solitary confinement causes Ian to mentally deteriorate—he begins cutting himself and ultimately spends eighteen solid years in solitary. He strikes up a correspondence with the woman he shot, and despite her pleas, "the courts ignored [her] call for a reduced sentence" (153). The third case is that of Antonio Nunez, who saw daily violence at home and within his gang-infested L.A. neighborhood. Antonio was shot in the street along with his older brother, who died. Traumatized, Antonio had several brushes with the law before becoming involved in a car chase and shootout at the age of fourteen. He was sentenced to life in prison for *kidnapping*, as the judge deemed him unfit to be rehabilitated. Stevenson connects these juvenile offenders to George Stinney, a black child accused of killing a little white girl. He was nearly lynched but instead was convicted by an all-white jury and executed 81 days after the crime had been committed. He was fourteen.

Chapter 9 Summary: I'm Here

"Finally, the date for Walter McMillian's hearing had arrived" (163). It took all of Stevenson and Michael's efforts to get Walter a hearing at all, and they know that the new judge, Judge Norton, is already tired of the case. They are most concerned with Ralph Myers testimony—he is erratic and odd, and of course, he's lied on the stand before. They do their best to prep him for testimony. Walter's entire community comes out to support him at the hearing, a fact that clearly annoys DA Chapman and Sherriff Tate. Myers testifies first. He tells the courtroom that his previous testimony was all lies—Stevenson notes with pleasure that Judge Norton is now listening "with rapt attention" (170). Myers' testimony is "direct and persuasive" (170).

On the second day of the hearing, Stevenson arrives on time to find all Walter's black friends and family barred from the courtroom. When he is allowed to enter, Stevenson sees that the courtroom now includes a metal detector and a German Shepherd police dog. The benches are filled with white people. Livid, Stevenson complains and some of Walter's supporters are allowed through. This includes Mrs. Williams, "an older black woman" (176) who, when she sees the police dog, cannot bear to enter the courtroom. After morning testimony, in which Myers' caretakers at the psych facility confirm his story that he was threatened into testifying against Walter, Stevenson encounters Mrs. Williamson in the parking lot. She reveals that she was attacked by police dogs at the 1965 Civil Rights march in Selma. The next day, Mrs. Williamson walks past the dog.

The most damning evidence comes during the third day of the hearing. Stevenson presents Ralph Myers' original interrogation tape, in which Sherriff Tate and others coercion of and threats against Ralph Myers. They confirm Ralph's current testimony and were not originally provided to Walter's original attorney, which is highly illegal. The

DA chooses not to rebut. The judge asks both sides to create written briefs to help make his decision.

Chapter 10 Summary: Mitigation

In this chapter, Stevenson explores how prisons have replaced hospitals as repositories for people with severe, often incurable mental illnesses. He explains that in the nineteenth century, activists such as Dorothea Dix pushed for the transfer of the mentally ill from prisons, where they were abused by guards and other prisoners, to hospitals and private mental health facilities. However, by the mid twentieth century, abuse at these long-term treatment centers had become commonplace, and activists were now concerned that the rights of the mentally ill were being violated. People who had not committed crimes could not be involuntarily held, they argued. This "deinstitutionalization" led to greater freedom for those with mental illnesses, but this freedom also led to greater rates of incarceration in prisons and jails, which were not equipped to treat ill people.

One of Stevenson's clients is George Daniel, a man who suffered a traumatic brain injury in a car accident and developed hallucinations and erratic behavior patterns. Before his family could get him medical help, he fled on a bus and ended up in a scuffle with an armed policeman. In the scuffle, the policeman was killed. Ed Seger, the doctor who examined George, determined he was "malingering" (190)—that is, faking his psychosis. George was given the death penalty for the cop's murder. As it turns out, Dr. Seger faked his credentials "for *eight years*" (190). Stevenson visits another mentally ill client, Avery Jenkins. In the parking lot, he sees a truck covered in Confederate flag bumper stickers and racist slogans. Stevenson is— against regulation—strip searched by the guard who owns that truck. In their first meeting, Stevenson can see how ill Avery is. Avery is unable to assist in his own defense, and just keeps asking about getting a chocolate milkshake.

At a hearing for Avery, Stevenson tells the court about the profound, traumatizing abuse Avery suffered while in foster care. He tells the court about how expecting Avery to live normally with no assistance was like expecting a legless man to climb stairs. Later, Stevenson encounters the strip search guard, who has been escorting Avery to the hearings and is now much kinder. The guard explains that he was also abused in foster care and appreciates what Stevenson did for Avery. He tells Stevenson he bought Avery a chocolate milkshake on the way home. Stevenson eventually gets Avery off death row and into a mental health facility. He later hears that the guard quit his job at the prison.

Chapter 7-10 Analysis

This section pays special attention to the people involved in criminal justice—guards, psychologists, and judges—and the power these players have in an accused person's life. Stevenson recalls one of his clients, Avery, who has severe mental disabilities. As such, he is completely at the mercy of the prison guards. The most brutal guard, who subjected Stevenson to a humiliating search and openly harbors Confederate sympathies, is by chance the one to accompany Avery to a hearing. There, he hears about Avery's severe abuse while in foster care. This same guard who openly hated black men such as Avery and Stevenson, suddenly sees a connection between himself and Avery, as the guard was also abused in foster care. This chance encounter allows him to see Avery not a prisoner, but as a human being just like himself. He later tells Stevenson that he took Avery to get a milkshake, something Avery had asked Stevenson for over the several months but Stevenson had been unable to bring him. When the notoriously racist guard goes out of his way to get Avery a milkshake, it is both an act of mercy and a return to his own humanity. He has spent years burying pain, by his own admission, and his decision to buy a black prisoner a gift represents the breaking down of these walls and barriers. Arguably, it is not a coincidence that he soon quits his job as a guard. Perhaps he began to see himself in the prisoners.

Mental health professionals, too, are complicit in the injustices perpetrated against marginalized people ill-equipped to defend themselves. The case of George Daniel is a particularly egregious example, with an unqualified medical professional making proclamations that forever affect George's life. But this ties back to the Walter McMillian case, as well—Ralph Myers was transported to a psych facility, only to have his doctors work closely with Sheriff Tate and others, rather than act in Ralph's best interest. It is clear from this section how the mental health field can align themselves with the criminal justice system, even when it is clearly to the detriment of their patients.

Finally, Stevenson's cases illustrate just how much leeway judges are given to determine the fate of accused criminals, and how unjust judicial decisions can have lasting consequences. In the case of Ian Manuel, the judge is so determined to incarcerate this child that he takes a relatively low-level offense—kidnapping—and uses his discretion to elevate this crime to a sentence of life in prison. And in Walter McMillian's hearing, the presiding judge is bored and dismissive of Stevenson's arguments at first, and even when he sees there is clear reason to overturn the verdict, allows for a metal detector and a police dog to be present in his courtroom, and for black supporters to be excluded. Even more than lawyers and the police, Stevenson makes it clear that judges wield extreme power over any given criminal case and are subject to the same prejudices.

Chapter 11-13

Chapter 11 Summary: I'll Fly Away

EJI experiences numerous threats over Walter's case—three bomb threats in two months, threatening phone calls, and racist letters. They persevere despite this. "We had work to do" (204). Judge Norton denies their appeal, which Stevenson half expected. Norton wants to be a "custodian" for the system, rather than dismantle it (204). Stevenson tells Walter not to lose hope—their best chance is yet to come, with the Alabama Court of Appeals. Michael moves on from EJI to work as a public defender in San Diego and is replaced by Bernard Harcourt, a young Harvard grad.

Stevenson debates whether to go more public with Walter's case. On one hand, Walter is being unfairly maligned, and the public has a right to know what a good person he is, how innocent he is. They also deserve to know about the abuses of power that have taken place. On the other hand, seeking media attention would open EJI up to defamation suits from Sherriff Tate and others. Stevenson decides to take the chance. He does interviews with *The Washington Post* and *60 Minutes* as he files his appeal with the Court of Appeals. There is immediate backlash from the local white community, but the black community is "thrilled to see honest coverage of the case" (212). DA Chapman, suddenly swayed by what he reads in the media coverage, secretly opens a new investigation into the case from his side. This creates a domino effect in which Bill Hooks recants his testimony and a new potential suspect is identified. Six weeks later, the Court of Appeals invalidates Walter's conviction and death sentence. Stevenson rushes to the prison to tell Walter, who reflects, for the first time, on all the time he has lost in prison. Walter is released as a free man the very next day.

Chapter 12 Summary: Mother, Mother

In this chapter, Stevenson highlights women on death row or sentenced to life in prison and the unique challenges they face based on their gender. The first case is that of Marsha Colbey. She was a mother of six living in a FEMA trailer and pregnant with a seventh (unplanned) child. Without insurance, money, or transportation for prenatal care or a hospital delivery, she gave birth at home. The baby was stillborn. Marsha buried him in the backyard, but this was soon discovered. The baby was exhumed and Marsha was charged with murder, as the medical examiner mistakenly concluded the baby had been born alive. She was sentenced to life in prison without parole.

At Tutwiler State Prison, Marsha was incarcerated with thousands of other women, most of them mothers. Some, just like her, had been convicted of murder after a stillbirth, imprisoned "for having unplanned pregnancies and bad judgment" (237). Tutwiler is dangerous for women—they are raped and harassed by male guards. With Stevenson and EJI's help, Marsha sentence is overturned and she is released after ten years of wrongful imprisonment. She is reunited with her children—one daughter clings to her, unable to let go even for a second.

Chapter 13 Summary: Recovery

After Walter is released, news of his story spreads. He is profiled in *The New York Times*. His conviction and eventual release are featured in *Circumstantial Evidence*, a book about the American justice system. Walter and Stevenson travel the country speaking about the case, and though Stevenson is frustrated by the inane questions and comments they receive (such as that Walter's eventual release only proves the justice system works) Walter continues on with "good humor, intelligence, and sincerity" (243). And yet, Walter is obviously damaged by his experiences. He has nightmares and grieves for his friends still behind bars. He receives no money in compensation for his ordeal, as per Alabama law at that time. Sherriff Tate continues to tell people Walter is guilty.

After a bitter, long-fought battle for civil compensation, Walter is awarded a small sum. Sherriff Tate is—as of the book's publication—still sheriff. After an accident, Walter takes on less physically demanding work. Stevenson starts teaching at NYU Law, and Walter is a frequent guest. But Walter's health is beginning to deteriorate—he is often confused and forgetful. During one interview with Swedish press, he becomes "uncharacteristically emotional" (254) and breaks down in sobs.

Chapter 11-13 Analysis

One major theme within this section is the role of media in demanding justice. Trials are often closed to local and national journalists, and few trials even warrant large media coverage. Stevenson is initially resistant to take Walter's case to the national media, who will surely jump on the story. He knows that publications such as *The New York Times* and *The Washington Post* will be seen as Yankee infiltrators by the Monroeville residents, who are understandably hostile toward outsiders telling them about their own home. And yet, Stevenson chooses to take the gamble. His worries are well-founded, as local media heavily criticizes the national media's take on Walter's trial. The black community, however, is relieved to see honest reporting of the case, for once. This presents an interesting dilemma—who has the right to report on cases like these? While national media was certainly favorable toward Walter, northern reporters are unlikely to grasp the full context of the situation. Local news would have greater context, but also greater bias. In the end, national, Northern media simply has more influence and reach. Their coverage spurs local authorities to reconsider their stance on the case. The national media coverage, despite any faults, is instrumental in freeing Walter. And once he is free, that same national media is instrumental in publicizing the real stories of wrongful conviction. Walter is generous with his time and tells his story over and over. He gives wrongful conviction a human face—even to his own detriment, as seen in the incident with the Swedish press. And yet, despite the reach and the audience of the national media, they remain unable to infiltrate Monroeville itself. Sherriff Tate is publicly, nationally branded a racist and liar, but is reelected to his post over and over. The effect of the national media is wide, but it is not always deep, and it cannot always change the hearts and minds of the very people on which it reports.

Chapter 14-Epilogue

Chapter 14 Summary: Cruel and Unusual

In this chapter, Stevenson utilizes the cases of several prisoners convicted as teenagers to show how life imprisonment for children is "cruel and unusual punishment." He begins with the case of Joe Sullivan, who at thirteen was coerced by two older boys into robbing an empty house. Later, one member of the group sexually assaulted an elderly white woman in her home, though the victim could tell which boy it was—all three were black.

The two older boys pinned the assault on Joe, and he was convicted after a one-day trial. Prison is hard on Joe, who is mentally disabled and becomes physically disabled due to the trauma of being raped by other prisoners. Stevenson takes the case and goes to visit Joe. He notes that Joe is extremely childlike.

Stevenson takes Joe's case as part of a larger effort to vacate the life sentences of people convicted as children, since the Supreme Court has ruled against the execution of such convicts. And isn't, Stevenson argues, death in prison analogous to a state execution? Two other cases include those of Ashley Jones, who killed abusive family members, and Evan Miller, an abused, suicidal child whose attempted robbery escalated to murder. Stevenson is impressed by the transformation these prisoners have undergone—they are thoughtful, reflective, and remorseful. Stevenson's own grandfather was murdered by two teenagers, but yet believes that young offenders deserve the chance to change. He notes the solid scientific evidence that teens lack "the maturity, the independence, and future orientation" (268) to be held responsible for crimes in the same way as adults. It is appalling, Stevenson believes, that we bar young teenagers from voting or drinking but are happy to incarcerate them for life. Stevenson takes Joe's case—and others—to the Supreme Court. As they await the verdict, Stevenson visits Joe in prison again, and as they talk, marvels "what a miracle it was that [Joe] could still laugh." (274)

Chapter 15 Summary: Broken

"Walter's decline came quickly" (275). He becomes increasingly forgetful and begins wandering without a destination. The diagnosis is advancing dementia, which will soon leave Walter completely incapacitated. Stevenson and Walter's family arrange for Walter to live in a facility—a difficult task given Walter's felony record. One facility agrees to take him short term. Stevenson, horribly busy trying to secure stays of execution for several men in Alabama, visits Walter there. Walter is at first cheerful but soon begins to panic, thinking the hospital is death row and begging Stevenson to save him. Stevenson calms him down. A nurse speaks privately to Stevenson about Walter, admitting that some of the staff is scared of him, given his time in prison. Stevenson reminds her Walter was innocent, but she says prison might *make* a man dangerous, even if he wasn't before. As he leaves the facility "shaken and disturbed" (280) he receives a call that despite EJI's best efforts, a client named Jimmy Dill will be executed.

Here, Stevenson gives background on the changing methods of execution in the US. The electric chair and gas chamber have been phased out in favor of lethal injection. This is seen as more humane, despite the fact that many of the drugs have been banned for *animal* use on the grounds they are too painful. Better drugs are available, but European suppliers, whose countries outlawed the death penalty decades ago, will not allow their products to be use to kill humans.

Jimmy Dill, Stevenson says, was part of an "unusual crime" (283). After Jimmy badly injured a man during a fight, the injured man's wife left him alone without proper care. The man died and Jimmy's crime was amended to murder. His lawyers did not inform him on a plea deal on the table, so he was sentenced to death. As Stevenson calls Jimmy on the night of his execution, Stevenson recalls a childhood memory. As a child, Stevenson laughed at a boy with a stutter, not knowing any better. Stevenson's mother ordered him to hug the boy and say "I love you." When Stevenson did, the boy responded, "I love you too." Jimmy tells Stevenson the same thing on the phone, even as he is about to die. Stevenson sees that he received such wondrous mercy from both Jimmy and the boy with the stutter. He resolves to keep fighting for mercy.

Chapter 16 Summary: The Stonecatcher's Song of Sorrow

In 2010, thanks to the tireless work of EJI and others, the Supreme Court declares life imprisonment without parole for children (who commit non-homicide crimes) to be unconstitutional. Two years later, this is amended to include homicide. Many people, including many EJI clients, are now eligible for reduced sentences. Stevenson now focuses his efforts on banning the housing of child offenders in adult facilities—regardless of protective custody or solitary living situations. Stevenson is gratified to see that executions in Alabama have decreased substantially. And yet, he is haunted by all the people he could not save.

Believing that a better education on racial discrimination will prevent future injustice, Stevenson launches a new initiative aimed at high school students. Stevenson splits "race in America" (he focuses on black Americans, here, as opposed to say, Native or Latino people) into four institutions. The first is chattel slavery, which black people could be sold into or born into. The second is the Reconstruction Era, which occurred directly after the Civil Rights and was marked by lynchings, disenfranchisement, and the rise of the KKK. The third was Jim Crow, in which racial discrimination and bias was institutionalized and defended fiercely. The fourth, Stevenson says, is mass incarceration.

Stevenson and his staff face difficulties in getting reduced sentences for those effected by the recent Supreme Court decision. In particular, they struggle to help inmates at Angola, once a slave planation, now a notoriously brutal prison/work camp. Two older men, Joshua Carter and Robert Caston, have been disabled by harsh manual labor in Angola but are now eligible for parole. Both men are released, to the joy of all involved. After one hearing, Stevenson encounters an older black woman in the courthouse. She is not involved with either man. Her grandson was murdered by two teen boys, and their life sentences only served to wound her more. She now visits the courthouse frequently to offer support to the families of victims and perpetrators alike. She calls herself a "stonecatcher," referring to the New Testament story of Jesus Christ halting the stoning of a woman and commanding the mob to look to their own sins rather than throw stones. She offers Stevenson a peppermint candy, which he accepts.

Epilogue Summary

In the book's short epilogue, Stevenson reflects on the life of Walter McMillian, who died in September 2013. He spent the last two years of his life living with his sister Katie. He was "kind and charming until the very end" (311). Stevenson attends the funeral and ponders all the shared anguish of the largely poor, black group of mourners. He takes comfort in the fact that Walter died as he wanted to—on God's schedule, not the government's schedule. He speaks to the crowd and tells them that among all the many things Walter taught him, the most important is this: "mercy is just when it is rooted in hopefulness and freely given" (313). Walter had mercy in his heart for all the people who harmed him, and it is because of this mercy he was able to make a life for himself after his release.

Chapter 14-Epilogue Analysis

One major theme of this final section is resilience—both the resilience of Stevenson's clients and of Stevenson himself. The Equal Justice Initiative, which could have easily collapsed many times, perseveres. Despite legal obstacles, hostile neighbors, and repeated bomb threats, EJI refuses to relent in securing justice for the most vulnerable Americans. And because of their resilience, they are able to make great strides. Thanks in part to their work, the Supreme Court declares life imprisonment without parole to be unconstitutional for minor offenders. Because of their dedication and refusal to cave under pressure, numerous men and women are released, granted new trials, or at the very least given good legal counsel. After Jimmy's execution, Stevenson drives home "broken hearted" but resolved to return to work the next day. "There was more work to do" (294).

Stevenson resilience is matched—arguably even surpassed—by that of his clients. In Chapter 14, he marvels at how mature and introspective his clients convicted as juveniles are. They entered a rigid, unfair system at a young age, but yet did not succumb to despair. They work to improve themselves and to forge identities separate from their crime and imprisonment. Jimmy Dill, even as he faces death, takes the time to thank Stevenson for all he has done. One non-client, the old woman Stevenson encounters in the courthouse, also shows remarkable resilience. Rather than lose herself in grief after her beloved grandson is killed, she channels her sorrow into helping others. While being present at murder trials must bring back horrible memories for her, she nonetheless sits through them, ready to lend her shoulder to others who are suffering. And finally, Walter McMillian is perhaps the book's strongest, most remarkable example of resilience. He holds no grudges against people who framed him and stole years from his life. After being freed, he gives his time to educating others. Even in the throes of dementia, he remains kind until the very last day of his life. In the last paragraphs of the Epilogue, Stevenson makes clear that Walter's resilience and mercy are things to be revered and emulated. Just as violence begets violence, resilience begets resilience. Because of Walter and the example he set, Stevenson will continue onwards and help more people just like Walter.

While there are many people—particularly clients—
mentioned in *Just Mercy*, few appear in more than one
chapter. Stevenson and Walter McMillian are the only true
"characters" of this nonfiction book, as the narrative is
centered around them, but we will also briefly mention
Ralph Myers and Sherriff Tate, who played central roles in
Walter's trial.

Bryan Stevenson

Bryan Stevenson is the book's narrator and central figure.
Over the course of *Just Mercy*, Stevenson progresses from
a timid, unexperienced intern to an accomplished,
dedicated lawyer, educator, and activist. Stevenson grows
up in a rural, black family in Southern Delaware. Despite
the technical dissolving of Jim Crow and legal segregation,
Stevenson's larger black community is "strong and
determined but marginalized and excluded" (13). His
family values education and the women of the family, in
particular, urge Stevenson to look outside his own
experiences. His mother is quick to correct him when he
laughs at a boy with a speech impediment. His
grandmother, the daughter of slaves and the family
matriarch, tells him that "'You can't understand most of the
important things from a distance, Bryan. You have to get
close'" (14).

Stevenson grew up in a rural black community, and this
connects him to many of his clients and their families.
While his adult life was marked by an elite education and
professional degrees, this does not erase his race or his
childhood class status. He was raised by people who lived
through the heyday of KKK, Jim Crow, and the Civil
Rights Movement. He feels a strong connection to others

who had similar experiences. When Mrs. Williams braves a police dog to enter Walter's hearing and tells Stevenson that she is present, he feels "A deep sense of recognition" (180).

Stevenson's early experiences inform his outlook and approach to life. Throughout *Just Mercy*, Stevenson displays high levels of empathy and a particular sense of fairness and justice. From the first time he meets a death row client, Stevenson approaches these men and women as human beings with rights and value to the world. Despite the fact that many of them have committed crimes—often murder—he consistently uses the word "we" in his narrative. Stevenson manages to see strong connections between himself and his clients. At one point, he states, "We are all broken by something... We all share the condition of brokenness, even if our brokenness is not equivalent" (288). Stevenson acknowledges his own brokenness and asks the reader to see theirs. From this, it is clear that Stevenson highly values the communal human experience and does not see criminality as something that erases a person's humanity. He is a tireless crusader for justice on behalf of marginalized people largely ignored by society. It is this innate, righteous thirst for fairness in an unfair world that drives his work. It is no coincidence that he chooses to structure his book around the Walter McMillian case. It is, at its core, a true and obvious injustice, the very thing Stevenson has devoted his life to fighting. On the eve of Walter's hearing, Stevenson resolves that Walter's innocence will be determined not by legal maneuvering, but "would be based on simple justice—he was an innocent man" (208).

Walter McMillian

Walter McMillian is a man wrongly convicted of murdering a white woman. He languishes on death row for years before the hard work of Bryan Stevenson and the Equal Justice Initiative frees him. After gaining his freedom, he travels the country speaking of his experience before tragically succumbing to trauma-induced dementia and dying in 2013. Stevenson, who spent many hours with Walter both during his imprisonment and after, describes him as a "kind, decent man with a generous nature" (103). He is, of course, not without his faults. His involvement in the murder trial stemmed from his affair with a younger white woman. He cheated on his ever-faithful wife and drank too much. And yet, for any bad decisions he has made, Stevenson and his family all believe Walter to be a person who consistently tries "to do the right thing" (104).

Walter is shown to be introspective and contemplative, and Stevenson acknowledges that his time in prison may have contributed to this. Without much to do, Walter escapes into his thoughts. He is concerned for the well-being of others, particularly his fellow death rows inmates. Each execution he witnesses makes him deeply sorrowful and physically ill. When he is finally freed from prison, he is anguished at having to leave the friends he has made. Even in his moment of greatest triumph, he is still thinking of those left behind.

After he is released, Walter channels his energy into remaking his life. He speaks at many events and to Stevenson's law students, something Stevenson is grateful for. Stevenson notes what a tremendous effect Walter's "personality, presence, and witness" (249) has on the students. When he speaks to groups, Walter is clear to state that he is not "angry or bitter" (249) about his experiences, something which displays great strength of character and an almost inhuman capacity for forgiveness, given the wrongs Walter has experienced. This is something that Stevenson remarks upon at Walter's funeral—his mercy. "Walter's strength, resistance, and perseverance were a triumph worth celebrating," Stevenson writes, "an accomplishment to be remembered" (313).

Ralph Myers

Ralph Myers is the chief witness against Walter in his first trial and the chief witness *for* Walter in the hearing to overturn Walter's conviction. Stevenson first describes Ralph as a "white man with a badly disfigured face and a lengthy criminal record" (31). Ralph has endured terrible hardships in his life, including a childhood in foster care in which he was terribly burned in an accident. He has emerged "emotional and frail," a "tragic outcast" who "craved attention," (31) which makes him an easily manipulated witness for the prosecution. He is coerced, bullied, and threatened into falsely implicating Walter in the murders. Ralph is not without a conscience and frequently tries to recant his false statements. For this, he is placed on death row, transported to mental facilities, and further threatened by Sherriff Tate and others. Ultimately, Ralph manages to redeem himself. Of his own volition, he contacts Stevenson and offers to speak on Walter's behalf. He is Stevenson's star witness at the hearing. He is "direct and persuasive" and his testimony is key in getting Walter freed.

Sherriff Tate

Sherriff Tom Tate is the corrupt, racist county sheriff directly responsible—along with many others—for Walter's wrongful conviction and imprisonment.

Remarkably, he shares a surname with the fictional Heck Tate, the sheriff in *To Kill a Mockingbird*. He is proudly provincial and never "ventured too far from Monroeville" (33). He is also unabashedly racist, spewing "racial slurs and threats" (47) at Walter during interrogation. Sherriff Tate is new to his position during the murders and feels intense pressure to close the cases. Because of this, he is willing to hide evidence and bully Ralph Myers into false testimony. Even when it is clear that Walter is innocent, Tate won't release him. "The arrest had been too long in the making to admit yet another failure" (51). He appears to have few scruples and is more concerned with his standing in the community than in truth or real justice.

THEMES

Institutionalized Racism

Stevenson, a black man, uses Walter McMillian's story, other cases, and his own experiences to paint a vivid picture of what institutionalized racism looks like in modern America. Walter's case involves clear instances of racism. He is first targeted by law enforcement due to his affair with a white woman. During interrogation, Sherriff Tate spews racial slurs at Walter and alludes to a horrifyingly recent lynching of a black man in Mobile, Alabama. This has the desired effect—"Walter was terrified" (48). Walter's trial is moved from a diverse area to a much whiter county so that there will be fewer available black jurors. As Stevenson mentions, "nearly everyone on death row had been tried by an all-white or nearly all-white jury" (60). The actions of white people involved in Walter's case—the sheriff, the judges, and the jury—were informed by racial prejudices. This racism institutionalized within the criminal justice system contributed to Walter's wrongful conviction.

The majority of Stevenson's mentioned clients are black. One client is convicted based on the testimony of a white witness who cannot tell three different black boys apart. Many have similar stories of being found guilty by all-white juries—juries that were hand-picked to be all-white. In one case, the available jurors were sorted into several categories—strong, medium, weak, and black. "All twenty-six black jurors could be found on the 'black' list, and the prosecutors excluded them all" (60). These machinations are clear examples of racism at an institutional level.

As a black man, Stevenson experiences racism and appalling prejudice, as well. He recalls in Chapter 2 being held at gunpoint by the police outside his own apartment building. He was simply listening to music in his car, but they assumed, based on his age and skin color, that he was there for nefarious purposes. At Walter's hearing, when black visitors are excluded from the courtroom, the court deputy tries to bar Stevenson as well. He sheepishly lets Stevenson in when it becomes clear he is Walter's lawyer. Stevenson recalls multiple incidents in which he is assumed to be a prisoner or defendant by white guards or judges. Based on his skin color, they automatically pigeonhole him as a criminal, rather than a lawyer. "The accumulated insults and indignations caused by racial presumptions," Stevenson writes, "are destructive in ways that are hard to measure" (300).

Justice

The first part of the book's title refers to the nebulous idea of "justice." In *Just Mercy*, Stevenson explores what justice truly means and what it looks like. In the Introduction, he places great importance on the idea of justice—rather than wealth, he says, "the opposite of poverty is justice" (17). As the book progresses, he shows with painful clarity how the most marginalized people in America—the poor, the young, the mentally ill, and racial minorities—are denied justice at every justice. Certainly, Walter McMillian's case is an obvious example of justice deferred. He is wrongfully convicted on a crime and spends years on death row due to a local sheriff's racism and pride. With Stevenson's help, he is eventually freed. But he has suffered for years. He has lost part of his life. Stevenson notes that "this miscarriage of justice had created permanent injuries" (222). Lack of justice, Stevenson argues, hurts more than the individual wronged person. In his closing statements at Walter's hearing, he feels a "simmering anger" at "how much pain and suffering had been inflicted on Walter and his family, the entire community" (224). This leaves open the question of whether Walter and the community received *true* justice. None of the men responsible for Walter's sham trial faced consequences. No amount of money could replace the years Walter lost. No verdict can heal the community-wide trauma.

Important to note is how differently the word "justice" is used by different players within the book. Prosecutors, sheriffs, and judges use the word to condemn people to lifelong prison terms and even death. For the larger criminal justice system, the word "justice" is something punitive. It refers to consequences placed on an individual for their crimes, real or fabricated. This is almost never what Stevenson uses the word to mean. When he speaks of justice, he refers to something positive given to an individual. As a criminal defense attorney, perhaps this is inevitable, but he also speaks of justice in a larger, systemic sense. When he speaks of "justice" for black Americans, he asks for equal protection under the law. When he speaks of "justice" for poor mothers or the mentally ill, he is referring to greater institutional support and care for these vulnerable populations. Justice means very different things depending on the speaker's perspective.

Mercy

The second half of the book's title refers to the less nebulous but no less important concept of mercy. As Stevenson notes early on in *Just Mercy*, "Each of us is more than the worst thing we've ever done" (17). One could read *Just Mercy* as a 300-page plea for mercy within the criminal justice system. While Walter McMillian is entirely innocent and therefore does not require mercy, only justice, many of Stevenson's clients are forthcoming about their guilt. They committed the crimes of which they were accused, but the courts were harsh and punitive, rather than merciful. Stevenson is quick to show mercy to his clients, not simply because he is their lawyer, but because they are human beings. "If you take something that doesn't belong to you, you are not *just* a thief. Even if you kill someone, you're not *just* a killer" (290). He continues, "When you experience mercy, you learn things that are hard to learn otherwise…You begin to recognize the humanity that resides in each of us" (290).

Each time Stevenson presents the reader with a new client and new case, he is careful to include the often horrifying details of the client's early life. Many clients were abused as children, or lost in the foster care system, or mentally disabled. Stevenson notes that frequently, juries were not permitted to hear this information, which may well have changed the outcome of the trials. While he asks for mercy for his clients, arguing that the tragedy in their lives stand as mitigating circumstances for their crimes, he also presents these circumstances as key to justice, as well. There is no justice is hiding a person's circumstances from the jury. Mercy and justice are inextricably tied.

In his eulogy at Walter's funeral, Stevenson speaks of Walter's ability to be merciful towards all those who had so wronged him. "And in the end, it was just mercy toward others that allowed him to recover a life worth celebrating" (313). In context, the phrase "just mercy" is purposefully ambiguous. Is it that mercy coupled with justice allowed Walter to move on? Or was simply—just—the act of mercy? Stevenson leaves the reader to determine that for themselves, but it is clear that Walter's tremendous capacity for mercy led to his remarkable life and continuing legacy.

To Kill a Mockingbird

As Stevenson repeatedly notes, Walter McMillian's trial and the fictional trial of *To Kill a Mockingbird's* Tom Robinson both take place in Alabama. Harper Lee's novel is something in which the white residents of Monroeville, AL take great pride, even erecting a museum to the book. Stevenson sees clear parallels between Walter and the fictional Tom Robinson. Both are poor, black men accused of crimes against white women. Both have obviously been set up as fall men for the true perpetrator, in order to appease the local white community. Both are convicted despite their clear innocence. And yet, the same white residents who all but worship *To Kill a Mockingbird* are quick to condemn Walter and assume his guilt. In this way, *To Kill a Mockingbird* represents the hypocrisy and blindness of the white community. They choose to revere a fictional tale of racial injustice while actively encouraging a real one in their very backyard. After a frustrating meeting with racist white law officials who seem determined to see Walter executed, Stevenson sees a flyer for a local production of *To Kill a Mockingbird*. This only adds to his "outrage" (108). The white members of this community prefer the fair defense of innocent black men to be relegated to Atticus Finch—not Bryan Stevenson.

Police dog

At one point during Walter's hearing, the police bring in a metal detector and a police dog. This is ostensibly to maintain order in the courtroom, but Stevenson knows it is truly to intimidate Walter's friends and family. He notes that "here in Alabama, police dogs and black folks looking for justice had never mixed well" (177) referring to the use of police dogs to intimidate and attack Civil Rights protesters. The police dog stands in for centuries of institutionalized racism and the very real multigenerational trauma of black Americans. Police dogs—particularly German shepherds, as this one is—are a recognizable element of the Civil Rights Movement, even for those who did not participate as Mrs. Williams. And it is because of this strong connection that the dog was brought to Walter's trial. The dog was there to intimidate the black observers, both those who were present at marches and sit-ins, and those who only heard stories. The dog represents the possibility of state-sanctioned violence. When Mrs. Williams walks past the German shepherd saying, "'I ain't scared of no dog!'" (180) she is really saying that she is unafraid of the white police officer handling the dog. She is no longer afraid of the people who have terrorized her and her community.

Music/Christian Hymns

In his narrative, Stevenson uses music—particularly Christian hymns—to show the raw inner feelings of his clients as well as himself. Several of the chapter titles are named after these Christian hymns, such as "The Old Rugged Cross" and "All God's Children." When Stevenson meets his first death row client as a lowly intern, he sees how terribly this man, Henry, is treated by the guards. Stevenson asks one guard to loose Henry's handcuffs, which are obviously too tight. The guard refuses and snaps at Stevenson. As Henry is being led out, he begins to sing a hymn called "Higher Ground," one that is well-known particularly within black churches. The lyrics, which speak of reaching new heights and ascending to a better plane—higher ground—are doubly important. First, Henry uses the hymn as a connecter between himself and Stevenson. He guesses, correctly, that Stevenson will know the song. And as a man condemned to die, he uses to lyrics to speak of his hope for mercy and peace in Heaven. Stevenson sees this song as a "precious gift" about "human potential, redemption, and hopefulness" (12). The first time he is with a client on the day of execution, a similar moment occurs. The client, Herbert, has said goodbye to family and to Stevenson. Stevenson, wanting to cry, begins to hum a hymn, instead—*The Old Rugged Cross*, a mournful hymn that Herbert had personally requested be played as he died. Herbert's family members begin to hum along with Stevenson. This hymn is centered around Jesus' cross—another state-sanctioned execution. The hymn represents all the mourners' unbearable sadness. It represents all the things they cannot say.

IMPORTANT QUOTES

1. "'Capital punishment means 'them without the capital get the punishment.'" (Introduction, p. 4)

   Early in the Introduction, Stevenson sets up one his central thesis statements for the book: that access to justice and the possibility of dying at the hands of the state are directly connected to a person's access to wealth. As his many case studies show, the poor are disproportionately affected by the justice system and death penalty. Many executions—particularly those of innocent people—could have been avoided if the prisoner had the money to hire a better lawyer.

2. "Each of us is more than the worst thing we've ever done." (Introduction, p. 17)

   Stevenson's experiences bear this statement out. Each person contains multitudes. One act, perhaps committed due to poverty, mental illness, or bad decision-making, does not wholly define a person. As the book progresses, the reader can see how this statement refers not just to prisoners, but to all involved in the criminal justice system. Many people make mistakes—not just convicted criminals, but sheriffs and judges, as well. And all people, Stevenson argues, deserve mercy.

3. "…the opposite of poverty is not wealth; the opposite of poverty is justice." (Introduction, p. 17)

   Here again, Stevenson draws a connection between class and justice. Wealth itself, he is arguing, is not the opposite of poverty. It is the access to real justice that poverty precludes *that is key. Giving people fair trials*

*and equal representation and treatment under the law
will combat poverty far more than any monetary
donation.*

4. "But there was no evidence against McMillian—no
   evidence except that he was an African American man
   involved in an adulterous interracial affair, which meant
   he was reckless and possibly dangerous, even if he had
   no prior criminal history and a good reputation"
   (Chapter 1, p.33)

   *Here, Stevenson suggests that far more than physical
   evidence, it was Walter's actions in the year leading up
   to the trial that made him a target. As he notes,
   interracial relationships were historically and continue
   to be sources of great scandal in the South. Walter
   chose to defy unspoken societal rules, and his defiance
   of these rules suggested that he could break others—
   even murder.*

5. "'Beat the drum for justice'" (Chapter 2, p. 45)

   *This is the command Stevenson receives from an old
   man who has heard him speak. The man is a former
   Civil Rights marcher who received scars from the
   police but calls them medals of honor. His words
   connect the historical Civil Rights Movement to
   Stevenson's continued campaign for the justice. It is
   new movement, but one that could not have existed
   without people like the scarred old man.*

6. "Walter thought the testimony was so nonsensical he
   couldn't believe people were taking it seriously. Why
   wasn't everyone laughing?" (Chapter 3, p. 66)

This is a horrifying moment for Walter during his trial. He sees, during Ralph Myers testimony, that his experience of the trial is not matching up with those of the white community. The white community is willfully choosing to ignore the obvious holes in Ralph's testimony. They have already convicted Walter in their minds, as he begins to see in this moment.

7. "'All this grievin' is hard. We can't cheer for the man you trying to help but don't want to have to grieve for him, too. There shouldn't be no more killing behind this.'" (Chapter 4, p. 81)

The family of a victim says this to Stevenson. They cannot be happy for the man Stevenson represents, but they do not want him to be executed, either. This statement bolsters Stevenson's central thesis that killing is a traumatizing, immoral act, whether it is a single person or the state doing the killing.

8. "I couldn't stop thinking that we don't spend much time contemplating the details of what killing someone actually involves." (Chapter 4, p. 90)

Stevenson, who has witnessed executions, has a perspective on capital punishment that few Americans have. Proponents of the death penalty rarely have the opportunity to witness an execution. They do not witness the pain of the condemned person's family. They do not watch the prisoner die—perhaps slowly and agonizingly. As such, they flippantly defend an institution they know nothing about.

9. "Walter's family and most poor black people in his community were similarly burdened by Walter's conviction...The pain in that trailer was tangible—I

could feel it. The community seemed desperate for some hope of justice." (Chapter 5, p. 101)

Throughout the book, Stevenson attempts to show how Walter's imprisonment was not only traumatizing the Walter, but to his entire black community. If Walter was taken from his home and his people, wrongfully convicted of a crime, and then might even be executed for it, the black community knows it could happen to them, too. If justice could be so denied to Walter, it could be denied to any of them simply because they are poor and black.

10. "The expansion of victims' rights ultimately made formal what had always been true: Some victims are more protected and valued than others." (Chapter 7, p. 142)

Stevenson acknowledges that it is not just defendants who are prejudged based on race or class. Victims, too, are ranked according to their place in society. He shows this through the community's differing responses to the murder of a prominent man's daughter as opposed to the murder of a rural, poor white woman. While the two share race, they do not share class, and the wealthier woman's case is given far more weight than the poor woman's.

11. "'I ain't scared of no dog.'" (Chapter 9, p. 180)

Mrs. Williams faces her fear of police dogs. She walks past what is essentially a symbol of institutionalized racism. She is no longer afraid of the systems that have oppressed her and the larger black community for hundreds of years.

12. "'I'm here.'" (Chapter 9, p. 181)

   *Mrs. Williams declares this to Stevenson. It is not
   simply a roll call. She is letting him know that she is
   present in the courtroom, but she is also declaring this
   to the judge, sheriff, and other white bystanders.
   Despite her fear of the police dog and the machinations
   designed to keep her out, she is in this courtroom to
   stay.*

13. "America's prisons have become warehouses for the
    mentally ill." (Chapter 10, p. 186)

   *Many of Stevenson's clients are mentally ill, and this
   mental illness often contributes to the crimes they
   committed. Stevenson details how the move out of
   institutionalizing the mentally ill gave individuals
   greater freedom, but ultimately, simply led to prisons
   becoming the new institutions.*

14. "'When is someone going to come into my courtroom
    and protect the rights of Confederate Americans?'"
    (Chapter 10, p. 193)

   *Stevenson hears the above quote from a Southern
   judge. This comment proves just how differently white
   Southerners and black Southerners can view the justice
   system. Despite having absolutely every systemic
   advantage, the white judge still sees himself as an
   oppressed class.*

15. "His freedom wouldn't be based on some tricky legal
    loophole or the exploitation of a technicality. It would
    be based on simple justice—he was an innocent man"
    (Chapter 11, p. 208)

Though Stevenson is an accomplished lawyer, he makes clear that this case is pure and simple—Walter did not commit the crime. No loopholes or complex arguments are even necessary. This is justice at its most basic.

16. "But the laughter today felt very different. It was the laughter of liberation." (Chapter 11, p. 221)

    Stevenson visits Walter in prison as he is about to be released. Though they have spent many hours together in this prison, the mood is noticeably different. After all their hard work, Walter is going home.

17. "In the last twenty years, we're created a new class of 'untouchables' in American society, made up of our most vulnerable mothers and their children." (Chapter 12, p. 236)

    Here, Stevenson alludes to the Hindu caste system's class of "untouchables"—people relegated by their birth to dangerous, unpleasant jobs and generally cast out of society, too lowly even to be touched by higher caste people. He argues that poor women—particularly minority or mentally ill women—and their children occupy that same place in American society. They are ignored and looked down upon, and when terrible accidents occur because of this societal abandonment, the mothers are viewed as villains and monsters.

18. "Adding insult to injury, Tate went on to be re-elected sheriff, and he remains in office today; he has been sheriff continuously for more than twenty-five years." (Chapter 13, p. 247)

    This is one of the book's most depressing realities. Despite Tate's many crimes, his overt racism, and his dogged determination to see an innocent man executed, he suffers no consequences for his actions. The white community of Monroeville continues to elect him year after year, placing him in a position of power which he could use to harm more people.

19. "Almost all the cases involved condemned people marked by the tragic irony that they were now nothing like the confused children who had committed a violent crime; they had all changed in some significant way." (Chapter 14, p. 266)

    Here, Stevenson is speaking of his clients who committed crimes as children. Unlike his adult offenders, these former child offenders have changed drastically since committing their crimes. And how could they not? Adolescence and young adulthood is a time of huge biological change. It seems horribly unfair to Stevenson that these clients' growth and maturity is not enough to grant them a second chance.

20. "We're supposed to sentence people fairly after fully considering their life circumstances, but instead we exploit the inability of the poor to get the legal assistance they need—all so we can kill them with less resistance." (Chapter 15, p. 287)

    All of Stevenson's clients are poor. Most have been badly disadvantaged by inadequate legal help, purely because they cannot pay for a lawyer's fees. Stevenson is appalled that the justice system is designed in a way to disadvantage the poor, even wrongfully convict them, purely so that they can be killed more easily.

21. "Why do we want to kill all the broken people? What is wrong with us, that we think a thing like that can be right?" (Chapter 15, p. 287)

On the eve of an execution, Stevenson experiences anguish as well as this moment of clarity. His clients—the ones who are guilty—are all broken people. They have been neglected and damaged by their parents, or foster care, or American society at large. Why, Stevenson wonders, is our response to this deep brokenness to kill them?

22. "But simply punishing the broken—walking away from them or hiding them from sight—only ensures that they remain broken and we do, too. There is no wholeness outside of our reciprocal humanity." (Chapter 13, p.290)

Here, Stevenson argues that violence only begets more violence. By killing or marginalizing people who are "broken," society only further breaks itself down. Justice and mercy are the only things that can bring a sense of wholeness as opposed to division.

23. "But today, our self-righteousness, our fear, and our anger have caused even Christians to hurl stones at the people who fall down, even when we know we should forgive or show compassion." (Chapter 16, p. 309)

Stevenson alludes to the Biblical story of Jesus Christ preventing the community-led stoning of a woman caught in adultery—arguably, the 1st century equivalent of a lynching. Jesus himself was a victim of capital punishment orchestrated by the state. Christians, Stevenson argues, have been complicit in throwing

stones despite their Savior making perfectly clear that
compassion and mercy must win out.

24. "The real question of capital punishment in this country
    is, *Do we deserve to kill?*" (Epilogue, p. 313)

    This question is the core of Just Mercy. *Through*
    numerous case studies and examples, Stevenson argues
    that not only is the justice system ill-equipped to
    accurately determine guilt and assess mitigating
    circumstances, but that it is morally wrong to kill a
    human being—no matter who does it.

25. "Mercy is most empowering, liberating, and
    transformative when it is directed at the underserving."
    (Epilogue, p. 313)

    This is Stevenson's final major point, delivered at
    Walter's funeral. Mercy is not simply designed for
    people like Walter, who were innocent and deserving. It
    is most important for people who are deeply broken and
    have committed great wrongs. Walter had mercy for the
    people who put him in prison and nearly executed him.
    He was merciful towards the undeserving, and this,
    Stevenson says, is what we all should emulate.

ESSAY TOPICS

1. *To Kill a Mockingbird* is, like *Just Mercy*, set in Monroe County, Alabama. Compare and contrast Harper Lee's novel with this nonfiction work. In what ways do the two works speak to similar themes of racism and the limits of justice? In what ways do works diverge?

2. The United States is the only Western country to use the death penalty. Behind China, it executes the greatest number of people each year. Consider why this might be. What about America's history or culture has allowed for this? What links does Stevenson draw between the death penalty and what it means to be "American?"

3. Stevenson presents the legal cases of both men and women, juveniles and adults. How does gender and/or age affect the cases he describes? Consider the standards of living, the prison "culture," and the inmates themselves at facilities for men vs. women and for adults vs. juvenile offenders?

4. Consider the childhoods of two of more convicts—what similarities do they share? Could something have been done in their formative years to prevent their incarceration? Defend your position.

5. What input, if any, should the families of victims have in deciding the fate of convicted criminals? Their wishes, as *Just Mercy* shows, are frequently taken into consideration. They are sometimes even present for executions. Should there be limits to their involvement? Why or why not?

6. Many people are involved in a single trial—a defendant, a judge, lawyers on both sides, and a jury. In your opinion and based on what you've read, who is most important element in a trial? Who truly decides a defendant's fate, and what are the limitations of their power?

7. If you could create a perfect justice system, what might it look like? How would you prevent or address the injustices and flaws presented in *Just Mercy*?

8. This book deals heavily with racial bias in policing, with officers treating black civilians—particularly young black men—with greater than suspicion than others. This has only become more apparent since *Just Mercy*'s 2014 publication. Consider more recent cases such as Philandro Castile, Michael Brown, Tamir Rice, and many others. What does Stevenson's work tell us about the reasons and mechanisms behind these? What does *Just Mercy* illuminate about a justice system in which the officers are frequently not convicted for these deaths?

9. What is the connection between money and justice? Stevenson believes that the opposite of poverty is justice. Do you believe this? Why or why not? In what ways does poverty *contribute* to injustice? Be sure to cite examples from the cases Stevenson writes about.

10. Consider the title. What is the relationship between "justice" and "mercy"? What does it mean for the law to be both just and merciful? Do any of the

cases in this book meet that criteria? Why or why not?

Made in the USA
Middletown, DE
24 December 2019